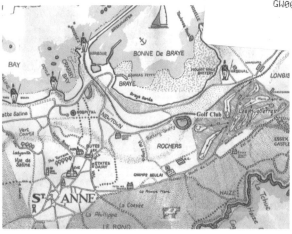

Alderney

A Little Souvenir

CHRIS ANDREWS

Alderney

West coast and Burhou

Foreword by

Sir Norman Browse
President of The States of Alderney

The Island of Alderney is unique. The only Channel Island truly in the English Channel, its mixture of people, town architecture and landscape reveal its mixed Norman-French and, since 1066, English heritage.

Getting here was made easy by the advent of the aeroplane - Alderney opened the first airport of the Channel Islands in 1935. In the days of sail, ships had to struggle through the fierce tides that run around our shores and many were wrecked. Once here, visitors can explore the Island's countryside, cliffs and beaches where they will find a vast variety of flowers and birds, or rest, on hot days, in the sunshine, on clear undisturbed sandy beaches; all beautifully illustrated in this book.

In winter (ours are warmer than those of mainland UK) the winds may challenge the cliff walkers but they are rewarded with stunningly beautiful, constantly changing views of the sea, clouds and sunsets. And after an energetic and lazy day, there are hotels and hostelries to meet everyones needs.

This book presents a taste of what you can find here. I hope you will come and visit us.

ALDERNEY

Alderney is an attractive island with a distinctive character. Situated some seventy miles to the south of the United Kingdom, but only seven miles off the coast of France, west of Cherbourg and in the English Channel (or *La Manche*). It is the most northerly of The Channel Islands, with Guernsey and Jersey away to the south west.

The Island is three and a half miles long by one and a half wide, the greater part open countryside; its charm is a mixture of the nature of St Anne, the major settlement with ancient cobbled streets and interesting buildings, and the spectacular sea and landscape of the largely unspoilt countryside outside the Town. The south and south-western coasts are

Guernsey cows on Alderney

mainly cliffs up to 270ft high, the northern and eastern coasts are lower and flatter with sandy beaches of varying sizes. There are numerous paths across the Island as well as rewarding cliff walks from which to see some of the 800 species of plants and 260 species of birds recorded here, many of them unique to Alderney or rare on the mainland.

The Island has a nature reserve looked after by The Alderney Wildlife Trust and a golf course in addition to all sorts of other attractions and is popular for walking, angling, birdwatching and sailing as well as traditional beach style

Platte Saline with Fort Tourgis beyond   7

Spring flowers and fields surrounding the Town

holidays. There are frequent summer events including an air race, fishing competitions and 'Alderney Week', the annual carnival with parties, competitions and parades to suit all tastes.

The main facilities, shops, hotels and restaurants are in the Town, a short steep walk up from the harbour, which as well as being the commercial port for the Island caters for visiting yachtsmen and ferries from France and the other Channel Islands. Visitors may also arrive by air, landing at one of the smallest commercial airports in the British Isles.

10   Fishing boat in the inner harbour

Alderney is a thriving community which encourages and welcomes visitors. It has a range of attractions throughout the season and this book attempts to show some of its unique charm.

12   Pretty houses and floral displays in Town

St Anne has many interesting historic houses as well as a variety of shops and restaurants 13

14   Houses in Newtown and along The Banquage above Braye Bay

The Town church, sometimes known as 'The Cathedral of The Channel Isles'   15

16 The house formerly owned by the famous cricket personality John Arlott

St Anne, Newtown and the Banquage from Braye Bay   17

18   Working fishermen in the inner harbour

The inner harbour   19

20 Gannet Rock

Fisherman at the rocks   21

22 Autumnal view of Braye from the east

East to the Lighthouse

26   Alderney Breakwater and Braye Bay from the Butes

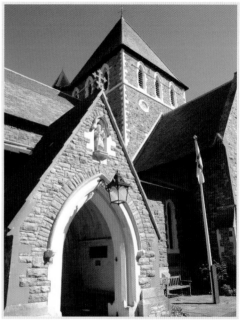

Clock tower of the old town church with the museum entrance, and the present day church   27

28   Fort Albert over Braye Bay

West coast cliffs in the autumn   29

30   Alderney is well known for its wild flowers, which grow abundantly, including in walls

Bluebells and white garlic flowers in spring   31

32   The golf course has spectacular views over much of the Island and surrounding seas

Hoary Stock at Crabby Bay and Fort Grosnez   33

34 Exercise of all types is catered for on Alderney – the football ground above the Arsenal

Once derelict, Fort Quesnard has been brought back to life and is now a private residence   35

36   Platte Saline and Burhou

Sunset over rocks to the west of Fort Grosnez   37

38 Sunrise, France may be closer than you think!

Snow is rare, but here etches the west coast against the sea   39

Pale sands and sweeping beach at Longis

42   Built in 1912 Blanchard Lighthouse is now automated

Western edge of the Island and Telegraph Tower   43

44   Disused railway lines on the Breakwater but the Island still has functioning trains

Alderney has its own car registrations, some particularly appropriate 45

46   Travel to the Island is often by plane, but adverts at the harbour show the sea route is popular

48   Alderney has been involved in many conflicts, this construction from the First World War

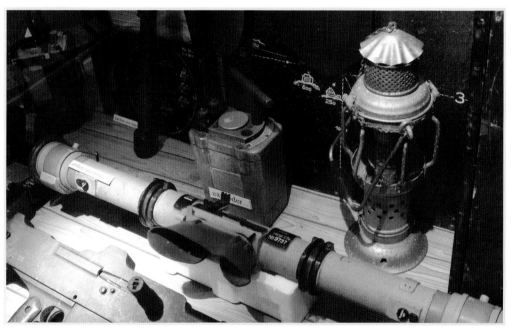

50   The Ile de Raz shows how over the years nature softens the wartime buildings.

Coaches from the London Underground form part of the current train   51

52   Nerines are a distinctive Channel Island bloom

Alderney is famous for its natural environment and wildlife, here Small Copper butterflies 53

54   Oystercatcher and the coast from the Ile de Raz

Cliffs and spring flowers on the west coast

58   Alderney Week, the annual spectacular celebrations

Junior section at the Salon Culinaire – a celebration of Alderney cuisine   59

60 Fireworks over the bay

A different sort of explosion! winter seas and the Breakwater   61

62   All in all Alderney is probably best known for its wide, safe sandy beaches, ...

Photographed and produced by Chris Andrews Publications

Tel: +44(0)1865 723404   email: chris.andrews1@btclick.com   **www: cap-ox.com**

ISBN 978-1-905385-17-1

Grateful thanks to The President, Sir Norman Browse for kindly contributing the foreword

Photographs by Chris Andrews. Additional material : Ian Laurence, Alderney Wildlife Trust and Joanna Parmentier. Endpaper Maps by David Manby   Front Cover: Fort Clonque and spring flowers,   Back Cover: The Harbour,   Title Page: Gannets.

Sales of this book help the Alderney Widlife Trust

This publication has been made possible by the generous support from: